Sales Techniques:
The Ultimate Guide To Yes

Spotty A. Bear

DEDICATION

Thank you for all those who believed in me and the idea of making the world better.. Whilst we can't explain bad things, we are forever changed for the bet

1 FAMILY

2 WEALTH

_____

_____

_____

_____

_____

_____

_____

_____

_____

_____

_____

_____

_____

_____

_____

_____

_____

_____

_____

_____

_____

_____

_____

_____

_____

_____

_____

_____

Spotty A. Bear

3 HEALTH

_____
_____
_____
_____
_____
_____
_____
_____
_____
_____
_____
_____
_____
_____
_____
_____
_____
_____
_____
_____
_____
_____
_____
_____
_____
_____
_____

Spotty A. Bear

4 SPIRITUAL

5 RELATIONSHIPS

_____
_____
_____
_____
_____
_____
_____
_____
_____
_____
_____
_____
_____
_____
_____
_____
_____
_____
_____
_____
_____
_____
_____
_____
_____
_____
_____

6 PERSONAL TIME

7 SPIRITUAL

8 FRIENDSHIP

9 . GRATITUDE

10. _____

ABOUT THE AUTHOR

Spotty A. Bear is the force that exists with all of us, the true ability and power to be the best we can. A force that truly believes in you and has a sense of awe and gratitude.

www.ingramcontent.com/pod-product-compliance
Lightning Source LLC
Chambersburg PA
CBHW061450180526
45170CB00004B/1643